THE RAINBOW CLUB INVADES PLANET EARTH

KC BROWNE

ILLUSTRATIONS BY
IVY MARIE APA

Copyright © 2013 by KC Browne. 303945-BROW
ISBN: Softcover   978-1-4771-0675-4
        Ebook   978-1-4771-0676-1

To order additional copies of this book, contact:
Xlibris Corporation
0-800-644-6988
www.xlibrispublishing.co.uk
Orders@ Xlibrispublishing.co.uk

The spaceship came whizzing out of the night sky. Rooku, Taasdii, Juuka and Shakie were stunned by the cosmos. They stood at the viewport gazing into space.

"Look, that's Earth there!" said Juuka with an enormous grin on his face.

"I wonder if it's like my dad said it is?" replied Rooku.

"I don't know? But we'll soon find out," Taasdii responded.

They all moved closer to the viewport, enthralled by the thought of finally reaching Earth.

All of a sudden the spaceship jerked sharply. The force of entering the Earths' atmosphere rocked them from side to side. The crew pulled themselves back towards the viewport. The sight of Earth grew larger and larger as each minute passed. Taasdii glanced at the control board and noticed all the lights were lit up. He started frantically performing some manoeuvres to regain control of the spaceship. He was bewildered as to what to do next.

"What's happening?" screamed Juuka.

"Are we losing control of the spaceship?" cried Rooku.

"Yes! I can't control it!" shrieked a frustrated Taasdii to his friends.

Rooku, Shakie and Juuka pondered on what to do next. The fear of crashing had turned their faces white. Shakie moved over to the control board.

"Let me try," said Shakie.

The spaceship sustained another jerk. All the crew fell onto the deck. The speed rapidly accelerated as the Earths' gravity pulled it nearer to Earth.

"Is everyone okay?" asked Rooku.

"Yes," replied Shakie, turning round to check if the other two were okay.

"My head hurts!" complained Taasdii.

"What are we going to do now?" Juuka stuttered.

"I don't know!" cried a baffled Taasdii.

They all looked at each other.

"Hurry up! We have to think of something quickly," demanded Rooku.

"Won't be long before we reach Earth," added Shakie.

They all went silent. Everyone started pacing the floor, trying to think of a solution. Juuka was the first to speak.

"I know what we could do!" he exclaimed, turning to the others.

"What?" replied Taasdii.

"We could all go outside and try to slow the spaceship down somehow," continued Juuka.

"Don't be stupid, we can't do that," retorted Shakie, trying not to cry.

"Well, you think of something then!" Juuka shouted back.

All went silent again in the spaceship. Taasdii walked back over to the control board. He stood there looking to see if he had missed any buttons. He glanced out of the viewport. They were getting nearer to Earth.

"We don't have much time left," he muttered to the others.

"Think everybody! Think!" wailed Rooku.

"We are thinking!" shrieked back Juuka.

Shakie jumped up in excitement, scaring the others in the process.

"Have you thought of something?" asked Taasdii, dashing over to him.

"Yes, I might have a plan," said Shakie.

"What is it?" Rooku eagerly inquired.

"I could glide down to Earth," he responded.

Taasdii, Rooku and Juuka stood there dwelling over the idea for a few minutes.

"Do you think that will work?" asked Juuka.

"It will," replied a persistant Shakie.

"Yes, only you know how to change into a handglider," stated Juuka. "You can fly us all down to safety then."

Taasdii stood staring at Juuka for a few moments. He wondered whether he'd be strong enough to carry them all.

"Yes, you're right, would be better if we all stay together," he replied.

They all rushed to the portal and Rooku opened it. The air rushed inside the spaceship nearly sucking them out. They clung onto the spaceship in desperation.

"Shut the portal!" yelled Taasdii to Shakie.

Shakie carefully moved to the portal. He eventually managed to slam it shut. All four stood there. Their bodies ached with the force of the suction.

"That idea's no good, we can't open the portal," said Juuka, his voice hoarse with breathelessness.

"We'll have to think of something else," uttered Shakie.

"Well, hurry up before the spaceship crashes!" screeched Rooku, taking another look through the viewport.

"Do you think we could just open the portal a bit so I can squeeze out?" inquired Shakie.

"I don't know, we could try it, I suppose," replied Taasdii. "You two open it for Shakie."

Rooku and Juuka walked over to the portal. They opened it slowly, just enough for Shakie to slip out. Shakie was sucked out, but managed to gain control of his body again. He altered shape into a handglider and flew around for a few moments.

The other three rushed over to the viewport. They stood there staring at Shakie flying around outside. He signalled that he was coming back for them. Taasdii dashed to the door.

"C'mon!" he shouted to his friends.

"Who's going first?" said Rooku.

Taasdii and Juuka looked at each other shrugging their shoulders.

"I'll go first," replied Juuka, unsure he was doing the right thing.

Taasdii opened the door again, Juuka squeezed out and jumped. His eyes closed for a split second. When he opened them he saw Shakie swooping down towards him. He hovered above Juuka who quickly reached out and grabbed hold of Shakie.

"Hold on tight!" Shakie yelled down to him.

As he circled back round he spotted Rooku and Taasdii through the viewport. They were jumping up and down pointing frantically. Shakie turned his head to have a look. He saw that they were too close to Earth. There was no time to help Rooku and Taasdii. He quickly turned tail and moved swiftly upwards away from them.

The spaceship hurled faster and faster towards Earth. Rooku and Taasdii were still stood at the viewport. Their faces etched with a horrified look.

"Quick, we have to try and escape, help me open the door," pleaded Rooku.

Taasdii shot after Rooku to stop him from opening the door.

"Don't be stupid! We don't have time to jump out!" he yelled back. Taasdii pulled

Rooku towards the back of the spaceship.

"Quick, change into something soft and find something to hang onto," he urged Rooku.

The spaceship landed with an almighty bang on Earth. The dust whirled around the spaceship like a sandstorm. Shakie and Juuka watched and waited a while for the dust to settle. It took a few minutes for their eyes to adjust to the darkness.

"Oh no!" cried an anguished Juuka.

"Hold on, we'll fly down and see if they are alive and okay!" yelled Shakie.

He swooped swiftly down as fast as possible. As Shakie and Juuka got nearer to the crash, a strong gust of wind blew them towards some trees. Shakie struggled to keep control, but clumsily landed in between the trees.

"Help! I'm stuck on the branches!" he shrieked down to Juuka.

"Wait, let me jump down then I can help you!" yelled back Juuka.

He quickly let go and managed to land safely on the ground. Juuka gazed back up towards Shakie and saw he was still struggling to free himself.

"What can I do?" muttered Juuka to himself. "I know, I'll change into something."

He paced the ground for a few minutes and then clicked his fingers together.

"Of course, a negunlie, they're small with sharp claws and big teeth, I can chew through the branches then," he softly whispered to himself again.

"I'm coming, hang on for a few minutes!" he shouted to Shakie.

Juuka shot up the tree with precise agility and began chewing through the branches.

"You're taking too long, do it faster," cried Shakie.

Juuka immediately made his head and mouth larger. He gnawed rapidly through the remaining branches. Shakie fell like lightning through the trees. He landed with an enormous thud on the ground.

"OW!" he yelped out.

Juuka rapidly rushed back down the tree to where Shakie was sat huddled.

"Are you okay?" he inquired.

"Do I look okay? Help me up," groaned Shakie.

Juuka bent down and lifted Shakie up. He stood there watching Shakie stretching his legs for a few moments.

"C'mon, we have to find Rooku and Taasdii," remarked Juuka.

They quickly moved towards where the spaceship was. As they got nearer most of the dust had settled. The damage to the spaceship shocked them. Juuka and Shakie swiftly started digging away the soil from the door. They both grabbed the door and pulled it open.

Shakie took a deep breath, praying Taasdii and Rooku would be okay. He cautiously stuck his head in and glanced around.

"Are they okay?" asked Juuka.

"I can't see them, let me go inside and check," Shakie replied.

Shakie carefully walked into the spaceship. His eyes scanned everywhere inside. They focused on a large pile at the back. He walked over to it and tried to look under it.

"Are you there?" he whispered.

"Help, we're stuck," Rooku said weakly.

"Juuka, come and help me, they're stuck under everything!" Shakie called out.

Juuka cautiously stepped over to Shakie. They both began to remove the pile off Taasdii and Rooku.

"Get Taasdii out, he's not moving," uttered Rooku.

"Quick, you get his legs and I'll get his shoulders," said Shakie.

After carefully laying him on the ground outside, Juuka went back for Rooku. Shakie frantically shook Taasdii in an attempt to wake him up. He eventually regained conciousness again. Juuka came back out, holding Rooku up.

"Is he okay?" asked Juuka.

"I think so," answered Shakie.

"I'll be okay in a minute, just need some time to rest," groaned Taasdii.

The crew sat down for a bit until Taasdii and Rooku were fit to walk.

"That was a bad crash," moaned Taasdii. "Look at the mess of the spaceship."

Rooku stood there in fear. He wondered what he was going to tell his dad when he got back home. He knew he would be in trouble for stealing the spaceship.

"My dad's going to be angry with me," said Rooku.

"Well I suppose we should try to find some help to fix the spaceship," suggested Juuka.

"C'mon you lot, let's move the spaceship, and cover it up before anybody sees it!" shouted Taasdii to the others. When they had finished this, they stood for a few minutes looking around them. They decided to climb over the hill in front of them. As they reached the top they spotted a building.

"Look there's some lights on!" Juuka exclaimed.

"C'mon, hurry up you three, let's see if anybody is down there!" yelled Shakie.

They started to sprint towards the lights.

"Wouldn't we be better transforming into something that can move faster," puffed Taasdii.

"No!" shouted back Shakie. "We might scare people too much."

"Look, it's a garage!" Juuka screamed out, as they got nearer to the lights. They started walking very slowly to the garage.

"Be careful," whispered Taasdii to the others. "We don't know who is in there or what they're like." As they neared the window, they ducked down so that they wouldn't be spotted. The aliens decided that only one of them would go up to the window. Taasdii stood up and said he would go and ask for help. He crept nearer and slowly stood up. He came face to face with a woman called Stella who was sitting behind the window.

"Can you help us?" muttered Taasdii in a faint squeaky voice. Stella looked up and shrieked, "Help! Help! Somebody come quick, there's a funny looking alien talking to me!"

A skinny man called Kevin, ran out from a door at the back of the garage. He was closely followed by Sam, the owner of the garage. Kevin reached Stella first.

"Where is it?" he asked.

"Over there. It ran off into the inspection pit where the cars are fixed," replied Stella. She was still shaking from the sight of the alien.

"I thought I saw some more following it," she continued. "We're being invaded."

Kevin rushed outside and ran towards the inspection pit, looking for the aliens. They had all taken cover behind some stacked boxes. As he approached the aliens, the boxes fell to the floor with a loud crash. Kevin flinched, he carefully walked to where the boxes had fallen.

"I know where you are. You might as well come out," growled Kevin. He waited a few minutes, but they didn't appear. Kevin went to the doors and locked them.

"I have you trapped now!" he shouted out. Kevin looked around him and found a big wooden stick. He stood there waiting for the aliens to come out.

"What do we do now?" asked Juuka, turning to the others.

"I know, I could distract him while you three sneak out of here," suggested Rooku.

"Okay," replied Taasdii.

Rooku sneaked out of hiding and stood in full view of Kevin. "Come and get me!" he yelled at Kevin.

Kevin rushed over to where Rooku was stood. Rooku was too quick for him. He transformed into a dark purple bowling ball. Rooku rolled himself towards Kevin and knocked him down. Instead of sneaking away, the other three aliens decided to rush up to Kevin.

They started making funny faces and horrible noises at him. Kevin recoiled back in fear and escaped back to the garage shop.

"Help! Let me in!" screamed Kevin.

Sam opened the door and yanked him back into the shop.

"What's happened?" Sam demanded.

"It changed shape and knocked me down," replied Kevin. Stella looked at him as if he had gone mad.

"Don't be stupid. You can't change shapes just like that," she snapped.

"There were four of them and they made funny noises at me. I thought that they were going to hurt me," continued Kevin. Suddenly there was loud banging. They all turned around, the four aliens were staring at them through the window.

"I was right, we are being invaded by aliens," gasped Stella, unsure at what exactly she was looking at. Sam rushed over to the window.

"What do you want?" he shrieked.

"We want some help to fix our spaceship!" Taasdii yelled through the window.

"Have you got any money?" demanded Sam.

"Money, what's money?" muttered Juuka.

"You can't have your spaceship fixed without money," growled Sam.

"We want our spaceship fixed now!" screamed the aliens. They began banging on the window again.

"Go away or we'll phone the police," warned Sam. He was starting to get fed up of the aliens' behaviour. The aliens took no notice of him. Kevin turned to Sam and asked, "Shall I phone the police?"

"Yes, hurry up," sighed Sam. Kevin rushed to the back of the shop and through the door. He phoned the police and told them what was happening. The police didn't believe him when he told them that there were aliens at the garage. They eventually got fed up of Kevin and sent a police car out.

When the aliens heard the faint siren getting louder, they became scared.

"What is that noise?" demanded Taasdii.

Sam pressed his face onto the window and said, "That's the police, they're coming to get you and lock you up."

Taasdii looked at his petrified friends, "Quick, we have to get out of here," Taasdii told them. "Run as fast as you can." The other three nodded in agreement and they all scurried away, back into the darkness. The police car pulled up outside the garage as the aliens disappeared from sight. Two police officers got out of the car. They slowly walked towards the window where the people stood watching them.

"You reported being threatened by aliens," bellowed Bert, the oldest of the two policemen. He was trying hard not to laugh at them.

"This is not funny," growled Sam.

"You're too late anyway, they scampered off when they heard the police siren," snapped Stella. The policemen apologized and carried on asking them questions about what had happened.

After they had finished writing down everything, Bert inquired, "Which way did they go?" Kevin pointed across the garage forecourt and into the darkness.

"Shall we look around and see if they are still nearby?" asked David, the youngest policeman. He turned to face his partner and Bert nodded to him. Bert turned to Sam and said, "We'll be in touch with you if we find any of them."

"It might be better if you stay inside and keep the door locked for a while," warned David. Sam nodded, he knew the police didn't believe them and wouldn't look for the aliens.

The aliens had stopped jogging and were now standing still. They looked around them to see which way to go next. All of them decided to carry on walking straight ahead and soon they saw some more lights far away.

Shakie turned to the others, "There must be some more people over there."

"Maybe somebody will help us this time," replied Juuka. When they finally reached the lights, they were upset to find that there was no sign of life anywhere.

"I wonder where we are?" sighed Taasdii. They all stood looking puzzled at the empty streets.

"I've seen pictures like this in some books. It looks like one of their towns!" Shakie exclaimed. The aliens stood talking for a while deciding what to do next. They all agreed to carry on walking until they could find someone. It wasn't long before they heard some faint voices, that became louder as they got nearer to the bank.

"There are more people in there," whispered Rooku to the others.

"We'll have to be very quiet this time and be careful we don't scare anybody," mumbled Taasdii. They walked around the bank and soon found a large hole in the wall. All of them stood there for a few minutes deciding whether to crawl through the hole or carry on walking around the town. They took a vote on what to do. Juuka was out numbered as the other three wanted to go through the hole. Taasdii went in first followed by Rooku, Shakie and lastly Juuka.

After they had all crawled through it, they stood still for a few seconds, allowing their eyes to adjust to the darkness.

Juuka nudged the others and whispered, "What do we do now?"

"Let's try that door and see where it leads to," muttered Taasdii, pointing to a door in the corner of the room.

They tip-toed towards the door and opened it very carefully. It made a small creaking noise, which sounded louder than it actually was because the bank was so quiet.

All of a sudden, they heard footsteps and voices approaching. They quickly closed the door, and scurried back into the darkness. All of them stood motionless hoping that they wouldn't be seen.

"Did you hear that? That sounded like a door creaking?" said one of the voices.

"No, I didn't hear anything. You're hearing things," the second person grunted.

"No I'm not. It came from over there," answered back the first person.

The aliens heard the footsteps stop just outside the door. The door burst open and they could see two dark figures stood in the doorway. They were holding torches, which were flashed around the room.

"I told you that you were hearing things!" said a voice that bellowed out.

"I know I heard something and it came from in here," snapped back the other voice.

One of the robbers shone his torch around the room again. "There's nothing here. C'mon, let's get back to Trevor and the money," the man sighed.

The door closed with a loud bang and the room was dark once again. The aliens slowly reappeared from their hiding place.

"Did you lot hear that? They have this money thing that we need," exclaimed Shakie.

"Let's follow them and get some of this money," suggested Rooku.

They all crept to the door and listened for a few seconds. Juuka opened the door and the aliens quietly sneaked out along the corridor. As they moved towards the voices, they became nervous. After what had happened at the garage, they didn't know what to expect from the men.

Shakie was the first to see them. He lifted his hand up to warn the others to stop where they were. He waved them forward and one by one, they stuck their heads round the door to see what was happening.

Taasdii spotted the desk and turned to the others and whispered, "Let's hide behind that desk and we can see better."

"Okay," replied Rooku. "But we have to change ourselves into something small."

"I know, we can change into mice," whispered Taasdii.

They quickly transformed into mice and scurried across the room towards the desk. One of the robbers turned around and spotted them.

"Look, there's green mice scuttling across the floor towards the desk!" he shouted to his two friends.

The one called Trevor turned around. He yelled back. "Don't be stupid. There are no such things as green mice. You're imagining things!"

"No I'm not, am I Steve!" replied Barry.

Steve, the third robber, walked towards the desk and bent down to look for the mice.

He stood back up and turned to face Barry. "There's nothing under the desk. C'mon let's get the money and get out of here," snapped back Steve.

Steve and Barry started back towards Trevor when they heard a faint noise.

"See, I told you I saw something dart under the desk," said Barry.

Barry started to walk back towards the desk.

Trevor growled, "Forget about the mice. We have more important things to do!"

"Okay, I'm coming! I'm coming!" Barry shouted back.

The three robbers carried on packing the money away into bags. Barry, Steve and Trevor were unaware that the aliens were watching them.

"What are we going to do now?" whispered Taasdii to the others.

"Don't know?" replied Juuka, "Let's see what they do with the money."

When all the money had been packed away, the three robbers moved into another room. The aliens scampered from behind the desk and followed them. As they crossed the polished floor, Juuka fell over, and made a loud thud.

"Ouch, that hurt!" cried Juuka, rubbing his arm.

"Be quiet," murmured Shakie a bit too loudly.

The three robbers turned around to see what the noise was and were shocked to see the four aliens. They stood paralysed for a few minutes staring at them in disbelief.

Trevor turned to his friends and shrieked, "What are they?"

"I don't know, but catch them before they get away!" yelled Steve.

The three robbers rushed over to try to grab the aliens.

"Quick, hide somewhere!" shouted Rooku. They all split up and ran to find somewhere safe to hide.

Barry chased Juuka as he shot across the room and headed towards the desk. He managed to grab hold of Juuka.

"Quick, over here!" he shouted to the others. "I've got one of them!"

Trevor and Steve rushed over to Barry, but Steve slipped on the slick floor. Shakie saw this and quickly looked around the room to see if there was anything he could use on Steve. He spotted the floor polishing machine standing in the corner of the room.

Shakie rushed over to it and pulled it to where Steve was still laying on the floor. He lifted the machine onto Steves' face. Shakie turned it on for a few seconds, and then lifted it off.

"Look what he's done to my face. It's all flat and shiny. I can't feel my nose anymore!" screamed out Steve when he felt his face.

Shakie laughed with glee.

Steve, even angrier, tried to stand up, but his head kept flopping over. After a few attempts, he decided to stay sat down. He waited for his head to return to its' normal shape. This only took a few minutes and when it had changed back, Steve jumped up and started to chase Shakie.

"C'mon here you little pest!" he growled, determined to catch Shakie.

While all this had been going on, Juuka had wriggled free from Barry. He darted towards Taasdii and Rooku. They had come out from hiding to help Juuka and steal the moneybags.

When Steve saw what they were trying to do, he shouted to Barry and Trevor to stop them. It was too late, they had already grabbed the bags. All three of the robbers started to chase three of the aliens around the bank. Steve soon stopped when he realized that they were too small and fast for them to catch. He stood there watching his friends still chasing them. Steve suddenly remembered that there were four aliens, one of them was missing. He looked around him and spotted Shakie near the door. Shakie was waiting for the others to join him.

Steve smiled to himself as an idea came into his head. He carefully made his way towards Shakie. Steve managed to sneak up behind him while he was busy watching the others.

He pulled out his gun, pointed it at Shakie, and shouted "All of you come over here or I will shoot your friend!"

All three aliens stopped and looked over to where Steve stood with Shakie. Barry and Trevor grabbed hold of Rooku and Juuka, but they noticed that Taasdii had disappeared.

A strange rumbling noise coming from behind Steve startled them. Steve turned around and was shocked to see that a small steamroller was moving towards him.

Taasdii had only changed himself into a steamroller and was heading for Steve. Steve turned to run away and dropped his gun as he slid on the floor. Taasdii spotted this and turned around towards the gun. He drove over it, breaking it into small pieces.

Steve watched as Taasdii moved to the other side of the room. He quickly shot to where he had dropped his gun. He looked down and crumpled to his knees when he saw what had happened to his favourite gun.

He picked the pieces up and glanced over to his friends. "Look what he's done to my gun, it's in small pieces," he cried. He slowly stood up and turned around to face Taasdii, who had now returned to his normal shape. "You're going to pay for this," he warned him.

"No I'm not," snapped Taasdii, who quickly sprinted away as Steve started to chase him.

Barry was scared by what he had just seen. "I'm leaving!" he screeched to his friends. He rushed to the hole in the wall and started to clamber through it. When he was halfway through he became stuck. He looked down at his body and the wall. He saw that the wall had altered, he could not escape. Barry didn't realize that Juuka had followed him to the wall and crawled in as well. He changed himself into the same shape as the wall and wrapped himself around Barrys' body. This terrified Barry even more as he tried to wriggle his way free. He soon gave up when he found out it wasn't working.

"Help me! Get me out of the wall!" he shrieked.

Trevor and Steve rushed over and both of them got hold of one of Barrys' legs and pulled hard.

Suddenly, Juukas' face came out of the wall. He made a large bellowing noise at them and growled, "Go away!"

This scared the two robbers, who bolted a few feet away from Juuka.

Trevor bravely turned around and yelled back, "We're not leaving without Barry!"

Juuka changed back to his normal self, laughed at them and scampered away to join the others.

Barry quickly climbed out of the wall before anything else could happen to him. He scurried away and joined his friends. They ran back into the room where they had left the money.

Steve shouted, "Just get the money and let's get out of here!"

"No, we can't do that," replied Trevor. "The aliens might follow us, we have to lock them up somewhere."

The robbers sat down and whispered amongst themselves until they came up with a plan that they all agreed with.

All three robbers stood up and made their way towards the aliens, who had split up again. The three robbers decided to chase Rooku. When they finally caught him, they tied him up and shoved him in the banks' large safe. Then they quietly hid in the shadows of the room. The robbers waited patiently for his friends to come and help him.

Rooku cried out, "Help! I'm tied up!"

One by one, his friends came out to help him. When all the aliens were in the safe, Trevor hurried over and slammed the door shut. The three robbers jumped up and down with excitement. They had finally caught all four of the aliens.

The aliens became angry when they realized that they had been tricked. They banged on the door and shouted at the robbers to let them out. All they could hear was the three robbers laughing at them through the door. The aliens soon tired of banging on the door and sat down on the floor.

"What are we going to do now?" cried Juuka, annoyed.

"I know, why doesn't one of us slide under the door and spy on them," suggested Tassdii, leaping up with excitement.

"Yes, and we could change ourselves into money and hide in one of the moneybags, they would take us with them then," added Shakie.

"That's a great idea," laughed Rooku. "I'll do it while you lot wait here and then I'll come back for you."

"No, I know what we could do," smirked Juuka. "We could all make ourselves small and sneak inside the bags together."

"That's an even better idea," said Rooku. "C'mon, hurry up before they get away."

When the three robbers had heard the aliens go quiet, they started to get worried.

"What do you think they're doing?" whispered Barry.

"I don't know?" muttered Trevor "But I don't like it. I think they're plotting something."

Barry turned to face Steve and Trevor and murmured, "Let's get the money and get out of here before they do something."

The three robbers started to pick up the moneybags between them. Then Trevor turned to Steve. "I've left the tools in the other room, you can come with me and help me carry them," he demanded.

"Okay," replied Steve.

"I'll wait here and watch the money until you get back," Barry added as they made their way towards the other room.

Barry became nervous, there was still no noise from the aliens and he wondered what they were doing. Unknown to him, the four aliens had already sneaked out. They had slid under the door and into one of the moneybags. The aliens quickly changed into money, and lay quietly at the top of the bag.

It wasn't long before the other two came back. "Have you had any trouble from them?" asked Trevor.

"No, they've been quiet," replied Barry.

"C'mon let's go before anything else happens," grunted Trevor.

The three robbers picked up the moneybags and walked back to the hole. As they were walking, Barry noticed that Steve was struggling with one of the bags. "What's wrong with you?" he muttered.

"This bag's very heavy," moaned Steve. "There must be more money in this bag than the others."

"Probably," sighed Barry.

The aliens let out a sigh of relief, glad that they had not been discovered.

Trevor was the first to reach the hole, he put down his bags and turned to the other two. "I'll crawl through first, and then you two can pass me the bags and climb through," he uttered to them.

"Okay," replied both Barry and Steve together.

The three robbers were happy when they finally reached the car and were inside it.

"I'm glad that's all over," moaned Barry.

"Yeah, I thought we would never get away from those aliens," agreed Steve.

Taasdii tried hard not to let out a loud laugh.

"What was that noise?" growled Trevor, turning to look at his friends.

Steve and Barry stared back at Trevor and shrugged their shoulders. Steve, Barry, and Trevor leapt out of the car in fear.

"There must be something in the car with us!" cried Barry.

They stood there for a few minutes wondering what to do. Steve cautiously went back to the car and looked inside. He paced around the car while looking through the windows. He turned to Trevor and Barry and shouted, "There's nothing in the car!"

"Are you sure!" yelled Trevor.

"Yeah," snapped back Steve.

Trevor and Barry strolled back to the car and looked through the windows. When they were sure the car was safe, they settled back into their seats. Trevor started the engine and off they drove to their hideout. The journey was quiet and no more strange noises were heard.

When they reached the hideout, they grabbed the bags and hurried to get inside the house. They threw the bags onto the floor in the hallway with a loud thud.

The bag with the aliens inside let out such a loud, "OW!" as it hit the floor.

Steve quickly turned around to see where the noise had come from, but there was nobody in sight.

He turned to Barry and asked, "Did you hear anything then?"

Barry looked at him and muttered, "No, why?"

"I thought I heard a noise coming from where the moneybags are," persisted Steve. He scratched his head and frowned whilst looking at the bags.

"Oh, you're just imagining things," snapped Barry.

Steve knew that he had heard something and strided over to the moneybags. He nudged each one of them with his foot, but there was no noise from any of them. Steve turned and went to join the others in the room. He heard Barry and Trevor laughing and making fun of him.

"I'm not imagining things. I know I heard a noise coming from one of those bags!" he growled.

"You're mad," mocked Trevor, joining in the fun. "There's nothing there in the bag, look I'll show you myself."

Trevor marched over to where the bags had been thrown, he bent over and looked through them one by one. He showed Steve the inside of the bags at the same time.

"See, there's nothing in any of them," he sniggered.

"Alright, I was wrong," sighed Steve, feeling such an idiot for saying something about it now.

"C'mon, we'll take the bags into the room and share the money out," suggested Trevor.

Unknown to the robbers, the aliens had already sneaked out of the bag and were safely hidden in a cupboard in the room. They sat huddled together watching what the robbers were doing.

"What do we do now?" whispered Juuka very quietly.

"I don't know. Let's just see what happens," muttered Shakie.

"Why don't we steal one of the bags, get our spaceship mended, and then we can tell the police where they are hiding," Taasdii suggested.

The other three nodded their heads in agreement.

"We'll wait until they move out of the room, and then we'll grab one of the bags," added Rooku.

All four aliens continued to sit patiently and watch the robbers counting out the money and sharing it between them. When they had finished, Barry stood up, stretching and yawning.

"Haven't you got anything to eat? I'm starving," he moaned.

"We'll all have something to eat. I'm quite hungry myself," replied Trevor. He also had a stretch and yawned. "It's been a very busy night for us," he continued.

The robbers went into the kitchen searching for something to eat. Taasdii shot out from the cupboard and grabbed one of the bags, which belonged to Barry. He heard footsteps coming back towards the room. Taasdii swiftly sneaked back into the cupboard. He shut the door, leaving a little crack open for them to see through.

The robbers came back into the room and sat down.

Barry was fuming.

"I can't believe you have no food in the house!" he yelled at Trevor and kicked the coffee table.

"Stop complaining, we'll order some food in. After all, we have plenty of money now," laughed Trevor, patting his bags of money.

"Yeah, what shall we have?" sniggered Steve, joining in with Trevors' laughter.

After a few minutes they finally agreed to have southern fried chicken and chips. Barry picked up the phone, ordered the food, and gave them Trevors' address.

"Make sure you remember this address," whispered Taasdii. "We might need it later."

"What for?" inquired Juuka, with a puzzled look on his face.

"You'll find out later," snapped Taasdii.

The food didn't take long to arrive. Barry leapt up when he saw the van come up the drive. He shot to the door, opened it, and eagerly waited for the deliveryman to reach him. He gave him the money and told him to keep the change for his tip. The deliveryman thanked him and walked away. Barry slammed the door shut with a loud bang. He shouted to the others and rushed into the kitchen to share the food out. Trevor and Steve joined Barry and they all sat down at the kitchen table eating.

After a few minutes, Barry stood up and returned to the living room. He sat back down and continued eating and watching the film. The four aliens spied on Barry for a few minutes from the cupboard. Shakie was becoming increasingly bored with being sat down all the time. His mind started to wander. He suddenly jumped up in excitement.

"Watch this. I'm going to have some fun now," he muttered

"Why? What're you going to do?" giggled Rooku.

Shakie slipped through the gap in the door and put his finger to his lips.

"Ssh," he whispered.

He changed into a small spider and sneaked up to Barry. He waited patiently for Barry to turn away from his food. Barry got up to pick up the TV remote and turned the channel over. While he was busy staring at the TV, Shakie, who had made himself even smaller, crawled under Barrys' chips and waited. As Barry got nearer to the bottom of his chips, Shakies' face suddenly appeared out of the them, he grabbed hold of Barrys' face and gave him a big slobbering kiss. Barry jerked back in shock, knocking his food over in the process. He yelled for Trevor and Steve to come and look at this. Shakie heard running footsteps coming towards the room. He blew a big raspberry at Barry and shot off under the sofa.

The other two robbers burst into the room.

"What's happened?" asked Steve.

"There was this horrible face that came out of my chips while I was eating them!" screamed Barry.

"What? Don't be stupid," laughed Trevor. "Don't tell me you're seeing things as well."

"No I'm not imagining things!" snapped Barry, his face now turning bright red.

Steve and Trevor stared at Barry.

"Don't stare at me like that! I'm not lying! I did see a face come out of my chips!" he yelled at them.

"Alright! Alright! What happened after this face appeared from your chips?" sneered Trevor.

"Whatever it was, it bounced out and went under the sofa," growled Barry.

He wasn't going to tell them about the kiss and the raspberry it blew at him. They would think he was completely mad.

All three robbers got down on their hands and knees to look under the sofa, but it was too dark to see properly.

"Go and get my torch from the car Barry," demanded Trevor.

"I'm not going out there on my own, it might attack me again," snapped Barry.

Steve stood up, "I'll go and get it, I'm not scared," he sighed and paced out of the room.

When Steve returned, he handed the torch to Trevor, who bent down again.

"There's nothing there," Trevor muttered.

"But I saw it go under the sofa," cried Barry.

"Give me the torch. I'll look under the sofa," Steve butted in. The two men stood glaring at each other for a few seconds.

Steve got down and he flashed the torch everywhere under the sofa, but could not see anything there.

"Trevor's right, there's nothing under the sofa," he said as he looked up at Barry and Trevor.

Barry snatched the torch from Steve, bent down, and looked himself.

"I know it went under the sofa," he muttered

"It could have moved somewhere else. Let's check the rest of the room," suggested Steve.

All three men spent the next half an hour looking for it.

The four aliens decided it would be best to move out of the cupboard. They made themselves very small again. They sneaked out one by one through the room door. Shakie was the last to leave and as he went through the door, Barry, who had stood up suddenly spotted him.

"Look, there's that thing I saw going through the door now!" shrieked Barry.

The other two looked up, but didn't see anything. Steve rushed to the door.

"Where did it go?" he asked Barry.

"I've just told you. It went through the door and into the hallway!" snapped back Barry, pointing and marching towards the door.

"Didn't any of you two see it?" he shrieked.

"No," sighed Trevor and Steve.

Barry stood at the door and looked into the hallway, but the aliens had disappeared again. The other two robbers had reached Barry and they all edged into the hallway. They looked from side to side, under all the furniture and in every room.

"Well, there's no sign of them. They must have got away," muttered Barry, letting out a sigh of relief.

Shakie, Rooku, Juuka and Taasdii had sneaked into the kitchen, taking the stolen moneybag with them. Taasdii saw the food on the table, he nudged Rooku with his elbow and pointed to the food.

"Let's grab the food, I'm starving," he said, mimicking Barrys' voice.

The others laughed, as Taasdii face changed to look like Barrys'.

"C'mon, hurry up before they come back," Rooku urged, as he turned to the others.

Taasdii rushed over to the table and grabbed what he could. They made their way towards the back door, but it was locked and there was no key in the door.

"What do we do now?" asked Shakie.

"Let's try the front door and see if we can get out that way," suggested Juuka.

As they moved towards the kitchen door, the robbers came charging in.

"I told you I could hear voices," sneered Barry, as he turned to the other two with a sly smirk on his face.

"Get them! Don't let them get away this time!" yelled Steve, as he lunged at the aliens.

All four of the aliens darted around to the far side of the table and stood there staring at the robbers. The robbers moved towards the opposite side of the table and glared back at them. Steve and Barry made their way around the table. Trevor stood static and waited for any of them to try to sneak under the table.

As Steve and Barry moved nearer to them, the four aliens slowly edged away from the table. They bumped into the wall behind them. They stood there frozen in fear, wondering what the robbers were going to do to them.

Barry managed to get near enough to make a grab for Taasdii, but missed him when he suddenly bent down. He scurried away under the table and Trevor made a lunge for him as well and missed. The other three aliens decided to make a dash for it. All four of them shot into the hallway, closely followed by the robbers. They split up, Taasdii and Rooku shot upstairs and Juuka and Shakie ran back into the living room.

Trevor and Barry followed Juuka and Shakie and left Steve to follow Rooku and Taasdii upstairs. They escaped into one of the bedrooms and saw a wardrobe in the corner of the room. Rooku nudged Taasdii and pointed to the wardrobe.

"Hurry up and get in there," he whispered.

They hid under the clothes at the bottom of the wardrobe.

"Be quiet and stay hidden whatever happens," Taasdii whispered. Rooku just nodded his head in agreement.

Steve crept along the corridor listening for any strange noises. He reached the first bedroom and slowly opened the door. He peeped in, but he couldn't see properly as it was too dark. His hand fumbled for the light switch, he turned on the light, there was no sign of the aliens. Steve tip-toed into the room. He swiftly moved towards the bed and looked under it, but found nobody hidden under it. Steve sauntered over to the wardrobe and looked inside it, it was completely empty. After checking the rest of the room, he walked out and shut the door firmly behind him.

The next door along was the bathroom. It only took him a matter of seconds to quickly look around it. He came back into the hallway and tip-toed towards the last door. He carefully opened the door. Steve knew that they had to be hiding in here somewhere. He sneaked in, shutting and locking the door behind him. Steve slowly moved around the room, carefully checking every nook and cranny. He turned around and spotted the wardrobe, he cautiously walked over to it. Steve stood staring at it for a few minutes. He leaned forward and flung open the doors expecting to see the aliens inside. Steve was stunned when he saw nobody inside it.

"Where are you? I know you're in here somewhere," he muttered to himself.

He stood there scratching his head, when he noticed the clothes at the bottom of the wardrobe. Steve bent over, grabbed the clothes, and threw them over his shoulder in anger. When he looked back down again he saw both aliens huddled together. Fear was showing in their faces.

"Now I've got you!" he sneered. He shut the door and locked it so that they couldn't escape. Steve hurried off to fetch Barry and Trevor.

Meanwhile, downstairs, Barry and Trevor were still looking for Juuka and Shakie. They had hidden back in the cupboard. Barry was just about to open the cupboard door, when Steve rushed in.

"I've found them, they're locked up in the wardrobe upstairs," he said excitedly.

Trevor and Barry followed Steve upstairs and into the bedroom. They stood there patiently waiting for Steve to unlock the door. He flung the door open and there sat Taasdii and Rooku. They were still huddled together at the bottom of the wardrobe. Taasdii and Rooku jumped up and tried to make a run for it.

"Quick, grab them before they escape!" screamed Steve.

As the robbers surrounded them, Taasdii and Rooku suddenly changed shape.

They turned themselves into two big black bulls. Steve, Barry, and Trevor stumbled back in shock. They turned and ran back towards the stairs. The sound of hooves thundering close behind them was ringing in their ears.

"Let's get out of here!" screamed Trevor.

The robbers reached the top of the stairs.

"Get out of my way!" Barry yelled at Trevor, who was in front of him.

"No!" Trevor snapped back.

Barry, desperate to get out of the house, shoved Trevor out of the way. This made Trevor trip up on one of the stairs. As he started to fall, Trevor reached out and grabbed hold of Barrys' arm. He pulled Barry down the stairs with him, they hit every stair as they went down. Steve who was following close behind them made the mistake of turning around to see how near the bulls were. He stumbled over Barry and Trevor. All three of them ended up in a big pile at the bottom of the stairs.

The bulls, who had now reached half way down the stairs, swiftly vaulted up in the air and charged at the robbers. The robbers covered up their heads and screamed out in fear, waiting to be squashed. After a few minutes, the robbers heard the sound of laughter. Barry glanced through his fingers. He saw all four of the aliens standing there laughing and pointing at them. He nudged his friends and told them to get up.

Trevor stood up and began shaking his fist at them.

"You won't be laughing if I get hold of you!"

Steve tried to calm Trevor down.

"C'mon let's just grab the money and get out of here," he sighed.

They shot to the room, picked the money up, and made a dash for the front door.

"Quick, get in the car and start the engine!" Steve screamed at Trevor.

Trevor fumbled for his car keys in his trouser pocket and got into the drivers' seat. He opened the doors for Barry and Steve, who hastily piled into the car throwing the moneybags in first. The car started up straight away. As they drove backwards out of the driveway, they heard two large thuds on the car.

Trevor turned around just in time to see Taasdii and Shakie holding on to the windscreen wipers. He drove the car faster, hoping that they would fall off. Taasdii and Shakie were determined to hang onto the car.

Taasdii had a bright idea, he whispered to Shakie. Shakie turned himself into a large, thick elastic band. He moved down to the side of the car and wrapped himself around the car. He made sure that the car doors could not open and nobody could escape.

While Shakie was busy doing this, Taasdii made himself very long and thin. He squeezed inside the car engine. When he reached the engine, he slowly made his way up the steering wheel. Taasdii wrapped himself around it as he went along. He reached the top of the steering wheel and very carefully tied Trevors' hands to it.

Trevor felt something crawling over his hands. He looked down and screamed out in shock when he saw what had happened. Trevor tried pulling his hands off the steering wheel. When this failed, he yelled to his friends for help.

Barry leaned over to Trevors' seat and snapped, "What's up with you now?"

"Help me! My hands are tied to the wheel! I can't move them!" he screamed back.

Barry nudged Steve and told him to climb over and help Trevor. Steve awkwardly clambered into the front seat. He tried to pull Trevors' hands free. This did not work though. Steve looked around the car to see if he could find anything that would help him. He opened the glove compartment and found a large screwdriver inside. Steve grabbed the screwdriver. He gently pushed it between the steering wheel and Taasdii. Then he grabbed hold of the screwdriver with both hands and pulled back hard. All of a sudden, the screwdriver broke in two. One of the pieces went flying into Barrys' face.

Barry growled at Steve, "Watch what you're doing, you idiot."

Barry put his hand up to his head where he had been hit. He looked at his hand, which was covered in blood.

"Now look what you've done. Pass me something to wipe it with," he muttered at Steve.

Steve looked in the glove compartment for the tissues he had seen earlier.

He threw them at Barry. "Here, use them for your stupid head!"

"Will you two stop arguing?" he moaned. "You're supposed to be helping me get my hands off the steering wheel."

"Stop the car. We could try using the wrench. That might work," Barry said.

"Of course, I forgot about the wrench," replied Trevor.

He tried to pull the car to the side of the road. Taasdii wouldn't let him and he turned the steering wheel the other way. They both fought to control the car. Trevor put his foot on the brake and the car came to a sudden halt.

This didn't stop Taasdii though. He stretched his body a bit further and reached down to the car pedals. To Trevors' shock the car started up again. Taasdii had took control of the driving. He pressed the pedals down even further. The car screeched as it speeded up.

"Do something or we'll crash!" screamed Barry.

"I'm trying! I'm trying!" yelled Trevor in horror.

Steve, who was still sat in the front seat, leaned over. He tried to help Trevor regain control of the car. The car sped faster, overtaking a few cars that were in front of them. They nearly hit a car that was coming the other way. This caused the driver of the other car to lean out of his window. He shook his fist and shouted something, which nobody could hear.

Taasdii abruptly started to slow the car down. The robbers let out a huge sigh of relief.

"That was scary," muttered Steve.

"Yeah, I'm glad that's over," replied Trevor.

When the car had slowed down enough, Taasdii gently turned it around. He headed back towards Trevors' house. The car started to speed up again.

"Here we go again!" screamed Steve, his face beginning to turn white.

Barry closed his eyes and covered them with his hands. He was afraid of crashing into another car.

It wasn't long before they reached the house. Rooku and Juuka were standing outside. They were waiting patiently for their friends to return.

"Keep them in the car!" shouted Juuka.

"We've phoned the police and they're on their way," said Rooku as he rushed up to the car.

Barry turned to his friends and said, "C'mon, we've got to get out of this car. I'm not getting arrested and going to jail."

All three robbers tried to open the car doors, but failed. Shakie was too strong for them. The sound of a siren could be heard in the distance. It got louder as each minute passed.

"That's a police siren! Hurry up we have to get out of here!" Trevor screeched.

All three robbers started to panic. They kicked as hard as they could at the doors. Shakie was still too strong for them.

Within a few minutes, two police cars pulled into the driveway. They stopped behind the robbers' car. The four police officers scrambled out of their cars. They rushed over to the robbers' car. The police officers stopped abruptly and stared in amazement when they saw Rooku and Juuka standing next to the car.

"They must be the aliens from the garage!" exclaimed Ian, one of the four policemen.

Shakie and Taasdii quickly returned back to their normal shape. The police officers stood there in astonishment. The robbers saw this and took their chance to escape. Bert turned around just in time to see them running away.

"Quick grab them, don't just stand there!" he yelled.

The other three police officers gave chase and soon caught all of the robbers. They handcuffed them, and split them up into the two police cars.

While all this had been happening, the four aliens had escaped back into the house and locked the door. Juuka grabbed the stolen moneybag. They ran to one of the downstairs windows. All of them stood rigid in silence, watching the rumpus between the police and the robbers. After the police had locked the robbers in the cars, they raced towards the house.

"It might be faster if we split up. You two go upstairs while we check downstairs," whispered Bert.

As they neared the front door, they heard the door unlock. All four aliens came rushing out, knocking over two of the police officers in the process. They stood back up and all four police officers chased after the aliens. The aliens decided to split up into two groups.

"You two go that way and Taasdii and I will go this way! We'll meet up later!" yelled Rooku to Juuka and Shakie.

The police officers split up and followed them.

Rooku and Taasdii raced down the driveway, onto the road and along the path.

Two of the police officers followed close behind. They found it hard to keep up with them and eventually lost them.

Shakie and Juuka had decided to run behind the house. They were followed by the other two police officers. They stopped suddenly when they came across a ten foot brick wall at the back of the house.

"Now we've got you," sneered David.

Shakie and Juuka looked at each other, smiled and nodded in agreement.

"Let's show them, they can't catch us," whispered Juuka into Shakies' ear.

The two aliens changed into large vultures. They flew towards the police officers and hovered above their heads for a few minutes. Then Shakie and Juuka flew away into the dark sky and out of sight.

While Shakie and Juuka were flying, they spotted Rooku and Taasdii walking on the path below them. They swooped silently down behind them. They made a loud clucking noise. Rooku and Taasdii turned around in fright. Shakie and Juuka were stood there, pointing and laughing at them. Rooku and Taasdii were glad to see their friends again. All of them were soon laughing and joking about what had happened to the robbers and the police officers. When they had finished telling each other what had happened, they sat down. The aliens started to plan their next move.

Back at the house, Bert and David were still in shock and stood there in awe.

"Did you see that?" said David.

When he got no reply from Bert, he turned around, fearing the worst. Bert stood there trembling, his face as white as snow. David nudged Bert with his elbow and repeated his question.

This time Bert answered with a weak, "Yes."

Both police officers stood there in silence staring into the night sky. The sound of running footsteps brought David and Bert back to reality. They heard the other two police officers shouting to them.

"C'mon," said Bert. "And don't say anything about the aliens flying away."

"Why?" inquired David.

"Because they won't believe us and they will make fun of us all night," replied Bert. They made their way to the front of the house and joined up with the other two. "Did yours get away too!" yelled Bert. He had noticed that the other two police officers were alone.

"Yes, they ran away into the street and we lost them," muttered Ian, as he paced towards them.

"Well we might as well take these three robbers into the police station," grunted Bert.

David got into the robbers' car. The other three officers split up into the two police cars. They followed each other down the driveway and onto the road. They drove towards the station. None of them noticed the car that was following them at a safe distance.

The four aliens had decided to come back. They had waited patiently for the police to get in their cars and drive down the road. Juuka changed himself into a car. The other three climbed inside Juuka and stared through the windows.

The police took the robbers' statements and locked them up. The four police officers started to tell everyone else what the robbers had told them. Most of them didn't believe the robbers' story and laughed about it.

"Aliens don't exist," muttered one of the other police officers. He was unaware that the four aliens were stood outside the window listening to what everyone was saying.

"Did you hear what they've just said?" remarked Juuka angrily. "We'll show them we don't exist."

"Yes!" shouted all the others together.

With that, the four aliens huddled together again. They made plans on what to do next.

Trevor had not been in the cell long, when he saw Juuka peering through the window at him. He let out a loud scream that pierced the air.

"The aliens are here!" he shrieked.

He jumped up and ran to the cell door.

"Let me out! Let me out!" he screamed, banging his fists on the door.

The sound of laughter made Trevor turn around. He forced himself to look at the window. Juuka stood there pulling faces and making horrible noises at him. Trevor heard a loud clanging noise behind him. He turned around to see Ian, stood at the door, staring at him.

"What's wrong with you?" grunted Ian, annoyed.

"Didn't you see it? One of the aliens was looking through the window!" Trevor shrieked.

"Stand back near the wall," Ian snapped.

He pulled the bolt back and opened the door. Ian walked over to the window. He looked through it, but could see nothing in the darkness.

"There's nobody there," he sighed. "Stop messing me about." he added as he moved back to the door. Ian closed the door with a loud bang.

Trevor crept over to the window and glanced out.

"But there was somebody there," muttered Trevor to himself.

The four aliens were laughing outside the window.

"Go on, you're turn now," said Juuka to the others.

"Alright, I'll try to sneak into one of the cells," sniggered Shakie. "You three watch out for anybody coming."

Shakie moved further down the building and towards the next window. He stretched his legs so that he could reach the small window that was open at the top. He gently pushed his head through the window. Barry lay fast asleep. Shakie pulled his head back out. He muttered to the others that Barry was in the cell.

"Watch this," he whispered. "I'll sneak up on him and wake him up."

Shakie stretched back up to the window. He carefully pulled himself up, and slid through to the inside of the cell.

Once he had landed safely on the floor, he silently slid over to Barry. He looked towards the window. His three friends were watching him. Taasdii mouthed quietly to Shakie to hurry up, but he was not quiet enough.

Barry woke up with a start and looked around him. His eyes caught movement at the window. Barry blinked twice, trying to focus his eyes on the window. He sat up in shock. The aliens were staring back at him.

"Help! Help! They're coming to get me!" he cried.

Shakie shot over to Barry. He put his hand over Barrys' mouth, hoping it would keep him quiet. When this failed, the other three aliens climbed into the cell to help him.

They heard the sound of running feet approaching the cell. The door flew open and in charged six police officers. They had their batons out ready. The police officers stopped abruptly when they saw the four aliens.

"What are they?" asked one of the police officers.

"What do you think we are," retorted Juuka.

"It's the aliens, grab them quickly before they get away," ordered Bert.

The police officers lunged for the aliens, but they weren't fast enough. The aliens managed to sneak under them and through the door. The police officers rushed out after them, locking Barry back in his cell. It was too late, the aliens had already disappeared.

"Spread out and find them," instructed Bert. "They can't be far away."

The aliens dashed around the police station looking for somewhere to hide. They moved from one room to another trying to avoid the police. The police were getting closer and closer to them. After looking in a few rooms, the aliens stumbled across the interview room that was used for the robbers. Taasdii was the first one to spot the moneybags. He stood there pointing at them.

"Look, the bags," he squealed with glee. "Let's hide in one of the bags again."

One by one they made themselves small. They silently disappeared into one of the bags. In the distance, they could hear doors opening and shutting and the sound of hushed voices. After a while, it went quiet. The police had given up looking for them and returned back to their normal duties.

The aliens sat huddled together inside the bag. They waited patiently for the right time to sneak out. They were just about to do this, when they heard more footsteps coming towards the room. They stopped outside the door and the door creaked open.

"I'll get the bags," said a man with a deep voice.

The aliens sat trembling in fear, waiting for their bag to be picked up. Suddnly, they felt the floor move away from under them. All of them knew that they were being carried out of the room. A few minutes later, the aliens were thrown down. They landed with a bump on top of the other bags. The door shut with a loud bang. This was followed by the sound of a key locking the door. The police officers stood talking outside the door for a few moments. Then the aliens heard the sound of retreating footsteps as they walked away.

"C'mon, I'll grab one of the bags and we'll get out of here while we can," said Rooku.

Taasdii led the way, with the others following close behind him. They reached the front desk. Taasdii cautiously looked round the door to see if it was safe to sneak out. He waved to the others to creep past, one by one. All of them heaved a sigh of relief when they finally reached the front door. They opened the door quietly and fled into the darkness.

The draught that came from the opened door blew across to the desk. This caused Shaun, another police officer to look up. He stood staring at the door with a puzzled look on his face. He came from behind the desk and walked towards the door. He peered through the door window, but there was no sign of anybody outside.

"That's strange," he said to Stan, who was stood at the desk.

"What is?" replied Stan, turning to look at Shaun.

"We must have ghosts. The door has just opened and shut," he continued, still staring at the door.

Stan shrugged his shoulders.

"It was probably just a strong gust of wind," he replied.

"Yes, more than likely," said Shaun.

He went back to the desk and carried on with his work.

The aliens didn't stop running until they were sure that they were out of sight. There was silence for a few minutes while they bent over gasping for breath.

"I'm glad we got away from them," said Juuka, still puffing for breath.

"So am I," muttered Shakie. "I thought that we were going to get caught."

Rooku stood there holding up the bag of money.

"At least we can get our spaceship fixed now," Rooku laughed.

"Yes, let's get back to the garage. I want to go home now," said Shakie.

The others all nodded in agreement. They were all tired and ready to go home.

The aliens made their way back towards the garage. They hoped that this time they would get some help. As they reached the garage, they hid behind a small wall. The aliens wanted to make sure that the garage was empty and nobody would see them. All of a sudden, they heard strange noises coming from behind them. They crept further into the shadows, trembling in fear. As the sounds came nearer, they could make out voices, one of them sounded familiar.

"That sounds like your dad," whispered Taasdii to Rooku.

"It can't be," said Rooku, glaring into the darkness to see if it was his dad.

"It is! It's my dad!" screamed Rooku.

All four of them raced out towards Rookus' dad.

"Look! All of our dads' are here! They've come to rescue us!" shouted Juuka.

After they had all hugged each other, everybody started to talk at the same time.

"Ssh, quiet everybody. We can't all speak at the same time," Rookus' dad bellowed over everybody else.

He turned to Rooku and his friends.

"Well, what's happened this time? How did you end up here?"

The four friends looked at each other, each waiting for one of them to start speaking. Taasdii decided that he would be the one to tell them. He told their dads' everything that had happened. His friends constantly interrupted him whenever he missed anything out.

When Taasdii had finally finished, Rookus' dad jumped up.

"C'mon, I think it's time we all went home," he said.

"Yes," Rooku replied wearily.

When they reached the spaceships, they noticed that both of them were secured together.

"Whose idea was it to steal the spaceship?" asked Rookus' dad.

"It was Rooku!" cried Taasdii, Juuka and Shakie all together.

"Oh, was it now!" replied his dad sternly. "Somebody's in trouble."

Rooku turned to face his dad. He knew that he was in serious trouble for stealing it. He lifted his head up and saw the smile on his dads' face. He sighed with relief when he realized that his dad was only joking.

The spaceship slowly rose and hurtled back into the night sky. Taasdii, Rooku, Juuka and Shakie moved into a corner of the spaceship. They sat huddled together whispering amongst themselves.

"Where's the moneybag we stole?" Juuka whispered to Rooku.

"Here," replied Rooku, pulling the bag from behind him.

"What shall we do with it?" whispered Taasdii to the others.

"I think we should save it for next time," muttered Shakie. The others nodded their heads in agreement and winked at each other.

THE END

CPSIA information can be obtained
at www.ICGtesting.com
Printed in the USA
LVIC06n2007261113

362915LV00014B/201